Filing Trends In
Mortgage Loan Fraud

A Review of Suspicious Activity Reports Filed
July 1, 2007 through June 30, 2008

Filing Trends in Mortgage Loan Fraud

A Review of Suspicious Activity Reports Filed

July 1, 2007 through June 30, 2008

Table of Contents

Introduction

Suspicious Activity Reports (SARs) provide a valuable tool for regulatory agencies and law enforcement seeking to isolate specific instances of potential criminal activity for further investigation and to identify emerging money laundering and terrorism financing trends. These efforts involve government agencies at the Federal, state, and local levels that are authorized by the Financial Crimes Enforcement Network (FinCEN) to access data derived from SARs.[1]

Following a significant increase in SARs on mortgage loan fraud in 2003 and 2004, FinCEN began focusing attention on such activity. The first in a series of reports was issued in November 2006 specifically describing trends and patterns revealed in mortgage loan fraud SARs.[2] Earlier FinCEN reports examined SAR data on a range of factors relevant to mortgage fraud among various business sectors, including: the most frequently reported mortgage fraud methods and schemes; businesses and professions, or "subjects," involved in suspected mortgage fraud; and the key indicators or "red-flags" of mortgage loan fraud of which institutions should be aware in designing and implementing their SAR reporting programs.[3]

This current report updates and complements FinCEN's earlier mortgage fraud reports by describing trends in SAR filings for the period of July 1, 2007 to June 30, 2008, with comparisons to the previous five years. This report is limited in scope to reports of suspected mortgage fraud submitted on Form TD F 90-22.47 (the depository institution SAR) – the form used primarily by banks as defined under FinCEN's regulations.[4]

---

1. For FinCEN reports and publications on the uses and value of BSA reports, see the FinCEN website, http://www.fincen.gov/news_room/rp/index.html.

2. *Mortgage Loan Fraud: An Industry Assessment Based Upon Suspicious Activity Report Analysis,* November 2006, http://www.fincen.gov/news_room/rp/reports/pdf/mortgage_fraud112006.pdf.

3. *Ibid.* See also *Mortgage Loan Fraud: an Update of Trends Based upon Analysis of Suspicious Activity Reports,* April 2008; *Suspected Money Laundering in the Residential Real Estate Industry,* April 2008; *Money Laundering in the Commercial Real Estate Industry;* December 2006, at http://www.fincen.gov/news_room/nr/.

4. 31 CFR 103.11(c). The depository institution SAR is filed by all depository institutions operating in the United States, including insured banks, savings associations, savings association service corporations, credit unions, bank holding companies, nonbank subsidiaries of bank holding companies, Edge and Agreement corporations, and U.S. branches and agencies of foreign banks. The Federal Housing Finance Agency (FHFA), which is the Federal regulator for Fannie Mae and Freddie Mac, has established a process for the companies to report possible mortgage fraud to FHFA, which in turn files depository institution SARs with FinCEN.

This report offers an overview of mortgage loan fraud SAR filings to assist regulators and other stakeholders in assessing certain trends on the detection and reporting of mortgage loan fraud. FinCEN will continue discussions with its regulatory and industry partners on how SAR data may enhance analysis of broader mortgage fraud issues. These discussions may provide additional insights into the significance of, for example: changes in the volume of certain types of reports; the types of filers responsible for the greatest number of reports; and the effectiveness of anti-fraud and anti-money laundering (AML) measures.

For depository institutions, this report provides further context in the experiences across the financial industry as a whole. The analysis builds upon FinCEN's earlier mortgage loan fraud reports which detailed vulnerabilities to fraud, examined different types of fraudulent activity, and identified "red flag" indicators of possible fraud. Providing such information can aid financial institutions in making their respective BSA compliance and reporting activities more efficient and effective in catching potential illegal activity before it occurs, as well as providing law enforcement with the information necessary to help support investigation and prosecution of criminals. FinCEN specifically seeks to help financial institutions learn from the experience of others as to ways to seek to protect the institution and its customers from being victimized by fraud. This most recent report aims to provide new insights as to how a variety of businesses besides the lending institution can play a role in the discovery of potential fraud.

Unique among Federal agencies, FinCEN occupies a position at the intersection where the mutual interests of law enforcement, regulators, and the financial industry converge. This special vantage point allows FinCEN to have a line of sight on suspicious financial activities across the nation and to identify trends and patterns that may not be visible to an individual financial institution or industry, nor apparent at the local or even regional level. While the BSA is most often associated with its considerable power to thwart money launderers, FinCEN intends to continually improve its expert analysis of the BSA data to provide early warning to the nation of incipient trends of fraud or other criminal abuse of the financial system. This report provides an example of the type of analyses of BSA information performed by FinCEN in carrying out its regulatory functions as well as in support of regulatory and law enforcement partners on a targeted or strategic basis.

Executive Summary

From July 1, 2007 through June 30, 2008, financial institutions filed 62,084 depository institution SARs reporting mortgage loan fraud. This figure constituted 9 percent of all SAR submissions for the period and a 44 percent increase over the preceding year. Mortgage loan fraud was the third most reported activity during this period.

Nearly 900 filing institutions submitted mortgage loan fraud SARs. Of these, fewer than 200 institutions submitted 98 percent (apr. 60,800) of the total. The top 10 filing institutions submitted 57 percent (apr. 35,400) of these filings, compared to 30 percent for the top 10 filing institutions of all SARs. The top 25 filing institutions of mortgage loan fraud SARs submitted 82 percent (apr. 50,900) of filings. Hence, there is a high concentration of a small number of depository institutions that account for most mortgage loan fraud filings, as compared to SARs generally.

With respect to the *volume of filings*, institutions noting their primary Federal regulators as the Office of Thrift Supervision (OTS) or the Office of the Comptroller of the Currency (OCC) submitted 47 percent and 36 percent, respectively, of all mortgage loan fraud SARs.

In contrast, with respect to *filing institutions*, a third of filing institutions reported the Federal Deposit Insurance Corporation (FDIC) as their primary Federal regulator, more than any other Federal regulator.

Filing institutions reported in 34 percent of reports that detection of possible mortgage loan fraud occurred prior to loan funding. This compares with the 31 percent rate for the 12-month period analyzed in FinCEN's April 2008 report, and the 21 percent rate over the preceding decade, showing that institutions have become increasingly vigilant in trying to protect themselves from and report suspected fraud.[5]

In addition to standard Bank Secrecy Act/Anti Money Laundering (BSA/AML) reviews, several other factors and secondary parties contributed to the detection of suspected fraud. The SARs reveal that a variety of businesses, besides the lending institution, were stakeholders or otherwise involved in the detection of suspected mortgage loan fraud. Filing institutions referenced repurchase demands and insurance, each in 8 percent of filings. Additionally, institutions referenced foreclosures

---

5. See *Mortgage Loan Fraud: an Update of Trends Based upon Analysis of Suspicious Activity Reports*, April 2008, http://www.fincen.gov/news_room/rp/files/MortgageLoanFraudSARAssessment.pdf.

and early default payments in 13 percent and 2 percent of filings, respectively. In particular, mortgage loan purchasers and providers of mortgage or certificate insurance and similar credit enhancement appeared to have a prominent place in the discovery of possible fraud, which likely contributed to the increase in repurchase demands and denials of certain claims noted in the SARs.

Methodology

The focus of this report is the filing of mortgage loan fraud SARs. Data reflect incidents of suspected mortgage loan fraud activities reported by depository institutions in SARs[6] and derive from SARs wherein mortgage loan fraud is reported as a characterization of the suspicious activity observed. FinCEN continues to conduct additional analyses on related suspicious activities observed in other types of SARs including those filed by financial institutions from other industry sectors, such as money services businesses, securities and futures, and casinos and card clubs.

This report presents data from filings during the period of July 1, 2007 through June 30, 2008 with comparisons to the previous five years. Prior to 2003, filing trends on mortgage loan fraud SARs increased at similar rates to other SAR filings. In calendar year 2003, however, SARs reporting mortgage loan fraud increased 77 percent over the previous year, and continued to climb thereafter at a rate of increase in excess of the overall depository institution SAR filing trend. For this reason, the report does not include data prior to July 1, 2002.[7]

In Part III of the depository institution SAR form, filing institutions may select the characteristic(s) of the suspicious activity observed, which includes "mortgage loan fraud" in field 35(p). Unless noted otherwise in this report, data is derived from SAR forms where mortgage loan fraud is specifically indicated in field 35(p). SAR forms that do not indicate suspected mortgage fraud in field 35(p) were not included in the research or otherwise reflected in the findings in this report. In conducting this research, FinCEN accessed the BSA database to identify SARs for the period covered under this assessment using the filing date found in the Document Control Number (DCN)[8] of those SARs.

---

6. The SAR form is available on FinCEN's website at www.fincen.gov/forms.

7. Data on trends regarding SARs from April 1, 1996 through March 31, 2006 is available on the FinCEN website in the 2006 report, *Mortgage Loan Fraud: An Industry Assessment based upon Suspicious Activity Report Analysis,* found at http://www.fincen.gov/news_room/rp/reports/pdf/mortgage_fraud112006.pdf.

8. A DCN is a unique number assigned by the Internal Revenue Service (IRS) to identify BSA documents received at the Enterprise Computing Center in Detroit, Michigan. The DCN numbering convention includes the date the reports are received.

The filing data used in the "Aggregate Trends and Patterns" part of this assessment draws from BSA database fixed field counts. For structured data (data contained in standard formats and fixed fields) such as secondary activities, a simple query may obtain this data. The most useful data for law enforcement purposes, however, often comes from the *unstructured* data in Part V, Suspicious Activity Information Explanation/Description (the "narrative" section), as it allows filing institutions greater flexibility to fully describe the suspected activity as they understand it. The "Trends and Patterns in Activities Leading to Initial Suspicion" part of this assessment is a summary of the conclusions drawn from reading and analyzing the narrative sections of a sample group of 1,050 SARs (1.7% of the total mortgage loan fraud SARs for the reporting period).

Aggregate Trends and Patterns

The following sections describe aggregate trends and patterns observed in mortgage loan fraud SARs. The sections include data on the increase in mortgage loan fraud SARs, SARs prepared by top filers, and statistics on filings based on the institutions' primary Federal regulators.

Mortgage Loan Fraud SARs

Section Summary: The volume of SARs reporting suspected mortgage loan fraud increased 44 percent during the 12 months of the period covered under this assessment, with 62,084 SARs filed between July 1, 2007 and June 30, 2008. These reports accounted for 9 percent of all SARs filed during the same period. During this period, mortgage loan fraud was the third most reported activity in SARs.

General Increases

Chart 1 illustrates the filing trend for SARs reporting mortgage loan fraud for the 6 year period July 1, 2002 to June 30, 2008 in 12-month intervals.

Chart 1

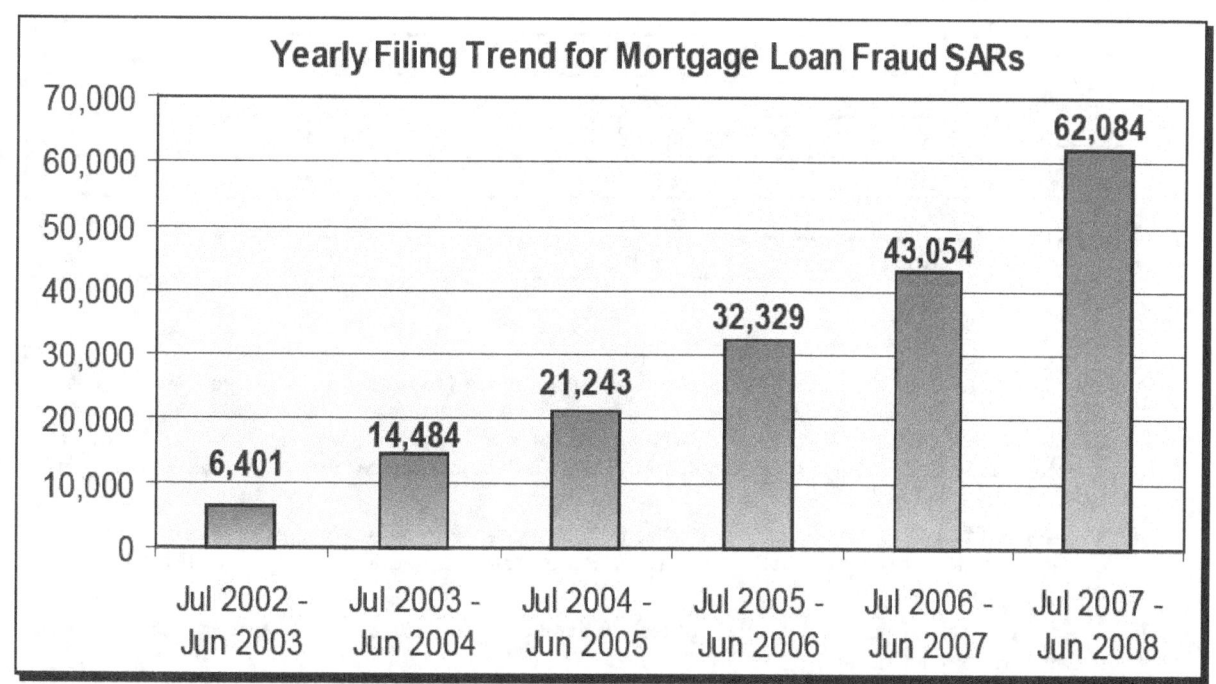

As seen in *Table 1*, between July 2002 and June 2008, depository institutions filed nearly 180,000 SARs with mortgage fraud as an activity characterization. Filings for the 12-month period ending June 30, 2008 increased 44 percent over the previous 12-month period. By comparison, all other SARs increased by only 9 percent.[9] While the number of mortgage loan fraud SARs increased significantly, it is important to note that the dates of the SAR filings are not always indicative of the dates of the underlying suspicious activities. Many SARs reflect activity dates that preceded the filing of the SARs by a number of years. Hence, an increase in the filings during this period is not necessarily indicative of an increase in mortgage loan fraud activities during the same period.

In the last 2 years of the review, mortgage loan fraud was the third most reported activity characterization on SARs. The three most reported characterizations, in order, were (1) the general category of BSA / Structuring / Money Laundering, (2) Check Fraud, and (3) Mortgage Loan Fraud.[10] *Table 1* shows the increase in mortgage loan fraud SARs in general and with respect to total SAR filings.[11]

Table 1

Mortgage Loan Fraud SARs - Yearly Increases and Percentages of Total SAR Filings			
Filing Date Range	*Mortgage Loan Fraud SARs*	*Percentage Increase*	*Percent of Total SAR Filings*
Jul 2002 – Jun 2003	6,401	22%	2%
Jul 2003 – Jun 2004	14,484	126%	4%
Jul 2004 – Jun 2005	21,243	47%	5%
Jul 2005 – Jun 2006	32,329	52%	6%
Jul 2006 – Jun 2007	43,054	33%	7%
Jul 2007 - Jun 2008	62,084	44%	9%
Total	179,595		6%

9. The statistic for "all other SARs" here reflects all SARs that did not include mortgage loan fraud as a suspicious activity characterization. The increase for all other activities should not be confused with the increase for all other reported SARs as many SARs contain multiple reported *activities*. Many of the other *activities* are also in mortgage loan fraud SARs, and, therefore, are not counted in the figure for "all other SARs."

10. The catchall "other" category for reported activity that does not fall into one of the specific categories on the depository institution SAR form was, statistically speaking, the second most indicated on the filings for the reporting period.

11. The filing increase for should not be confused with all other reported *activities*, as many filings contain multiple reported activities.

Comparison to Other SARs

Chart 2 shows the growth rate for mortgage loan fraud SARs compared to SAR filings which do not have this activity characterization.

Chart 2

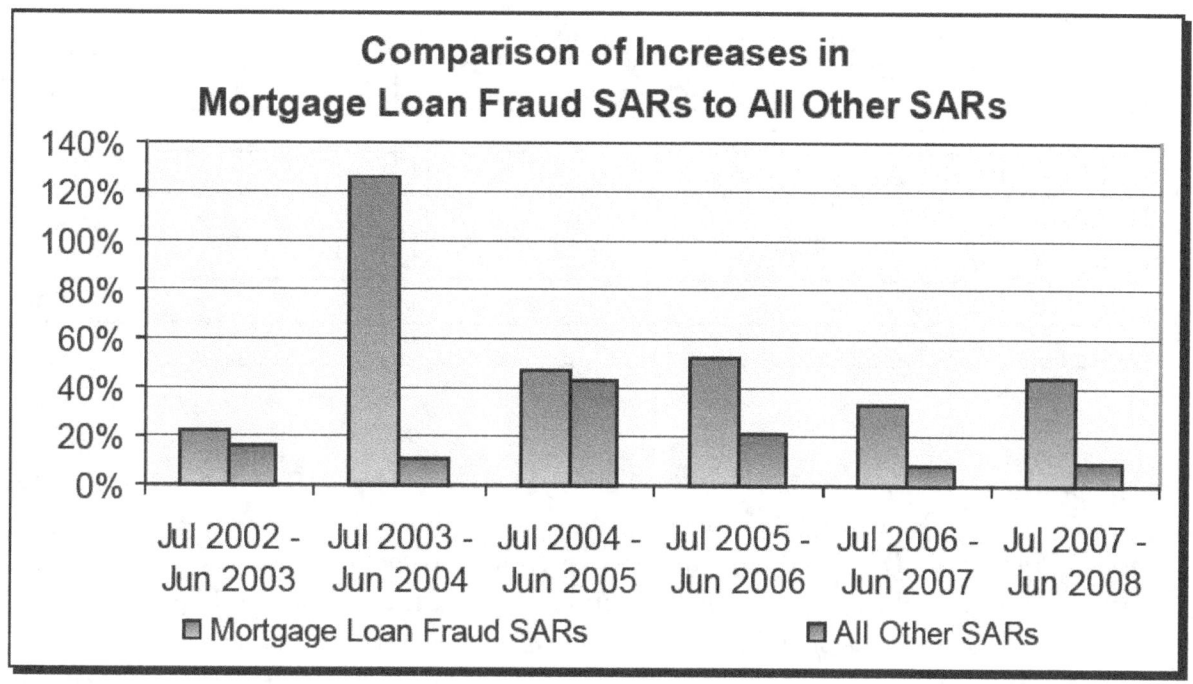

As seen in *Table 2*, the growth rate of mortgage loan fraud SARs outpaced that of all other SARs over each of the past 6 annual periods, often by a considerable amount.

Table 2

Comparison of Increases in Mortgage Loan Fraud SARs to All Other SARs		
Filing Date Range	*Mortgage Loan Fraud SARs - Filing Increases*	*Non-Mortgage Loan Fraud SARs – Filing Increases*
Jul 2002 - Jun 2003	22%	16%
Jul 2003 - Jun 2004	126%	11%
Jul 2004 - Jun 2005	47%	43%
Jul 2005 - Jun 2006	52%	21%
Jul 2006 - Jun 2007	33%	8%
Jul 2007 - Jun 2008	44%	9%

Filing Institutions

Section Summary: The top 10 filing institutions of SARs reporting suspected mortgage loan fraud submitted 57 percent of the total of such reports, whereas the top 10 filing institutions for SARs in general submitted 30 percent of all SARs. The top 25 filing institutions on suspected mortgage loan fraud submitted 82 percent of the total. Six filing institutions accounted for 36 percent of all mortgage loan fraud SARs but only one percent of all other SARs. Hence, mortgage loan fraud filings come predominantly from a more concentrated group of depository institutions than do SARs generally.

In a 12-month period, fewer than 200 depository institutions submitted the bulk of SARs (98 percent) with mortgage fraud as an activity characterization. Although nearly 900 institutions filed SARs reporting suspected mortgage loan fraud between July 1, 2007 and June 30, 2008, more than 700 of these institutions each filed fewer than five SARs with this characterization.[12] As *Chart 3* shows, the 25 top filing institutions of mortgage loan fraud SARs submitted 82 percent of the total 62,084 reports during this period.

---

12. The filer count is based on unique filer Employer Identification Numbers (EINs) reported in the SAR. As some businesses may use the same EIN for multiple branches or process all SARs at centralized locations for the entire organization, the total does not represent individual filer branch locations, but rather unique filer institutions. Although records reflect 987 EINs and 1,058 filer names, the total appears to be closer to 900 unique filers according to reported EINs, after taking into account typographical errors.

Chart 3

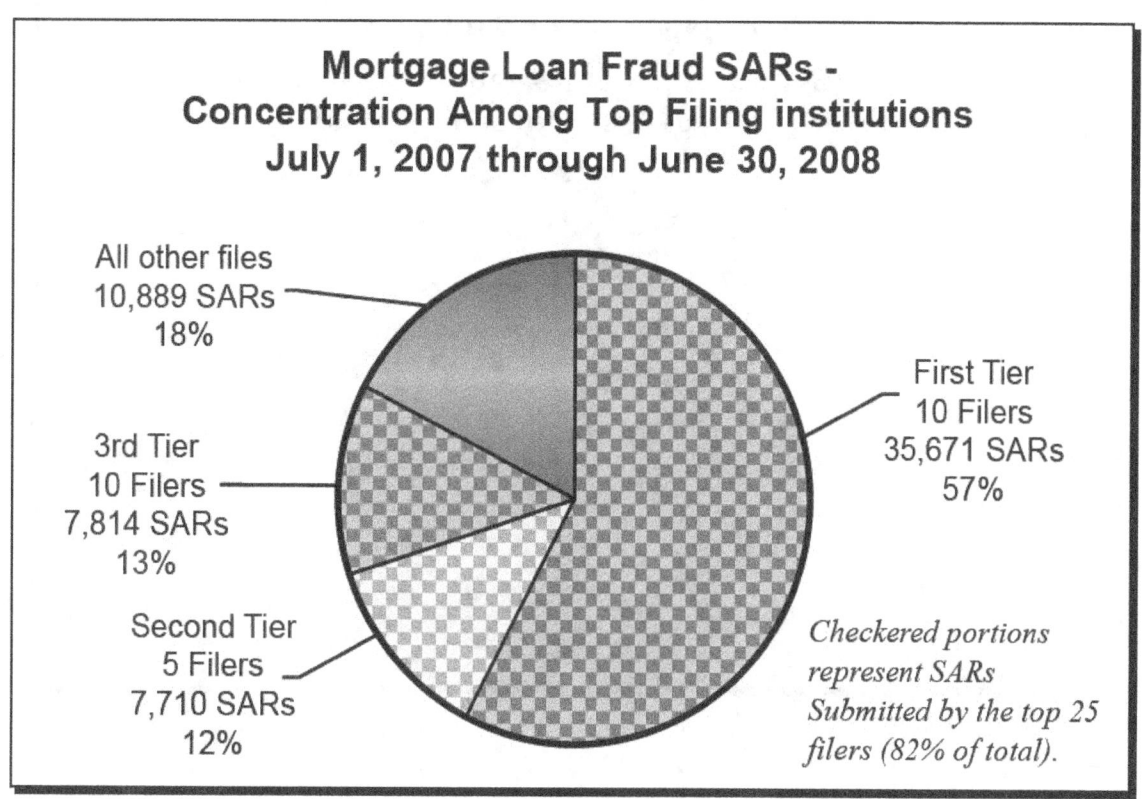

Mortgage Loan Fraud SARs - Concentration Among Top Filing institutions July 1, 2007 through June 30, 2008

All other files
10,889 SARs
18%

3rd Tier
10 Filers
7,814 SARs
13%

Second Tier
5 Filers
7,710 SARs
12%

First Tier
10 Filers
35,671 SARs
57%

Checkered portions represent SARs Submitted by the top 25 filers (82% of total).

The top 10 filing institutions of mortgage loan fraud SARs submitted 57 percent of these records. This concentration of submissions among the top filing institutions was notable compared to overall SAR filing trends. In contrast, the top 10 filing institutions for *all SARs* submitted 30 percent of the total records. *Charts 4* and *5* illustrate this difference.

Chart 4

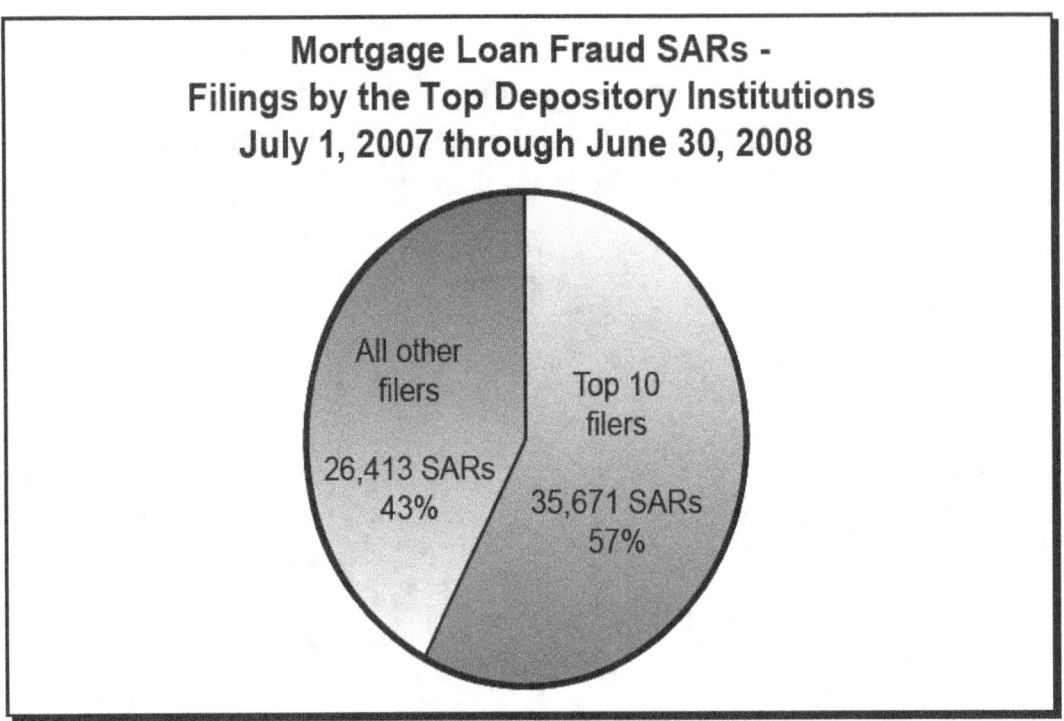

**Mortgage Loan Fraud SARs -
Filings by the Top Depository Institutions
July 1, 2007 through June 30, 2008**

All other filers

26,413 SARs
43%

Top 10 filers

35,671 SARs
57%

Chart 5

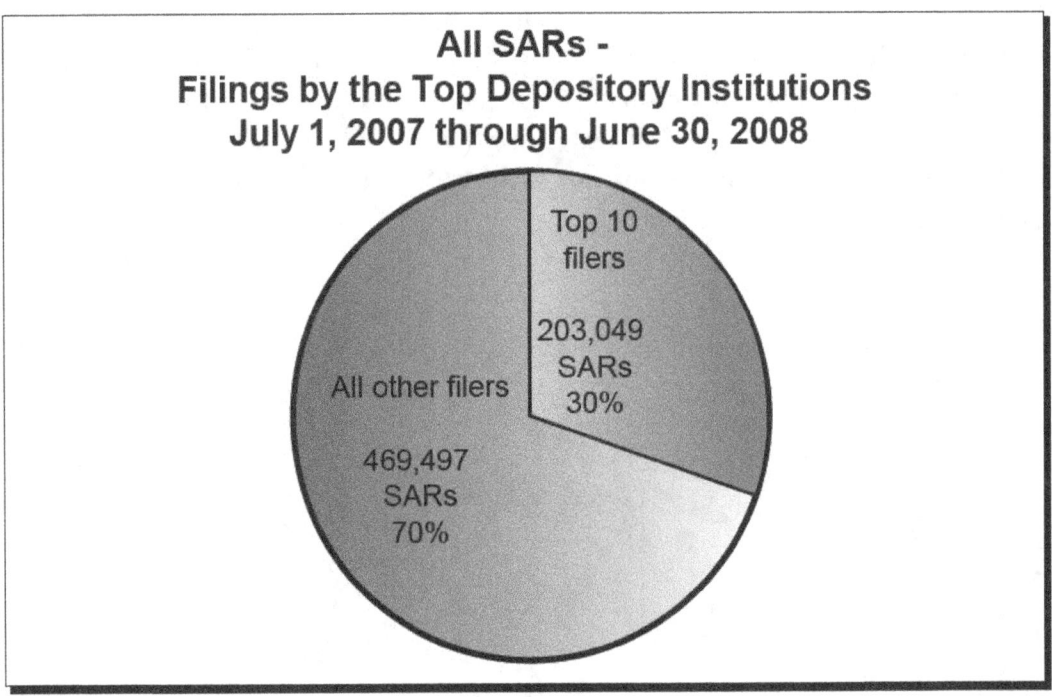

**All SARs -
Filings by the Top Depository Institutions
July 1, 2007 through June 30, 2008**

Top 10 filers

203,049 SARs
30%

All other filers

469,497 SARs
70%

Four of the top ten filing institutions of mortgage loan fraud SARs were also among the top ten filing institutions for all SARs irrespective of activity characterization. The remaining six filing institutions of this group accounted for 36 percent of all mortgage fraud filings but only 1 percent of all other SARs.[13] This would appear to be explained in part by the business model of those latter six filing institutions being relatively more focused on mortgage activity.

Primary Federal Regulators of Filing Institutions

Section Summary: In terms of total SARs, institutions that identified the Office of Thrift Supervision (OTS) and the Office of the Comptroller of the Currency (OCC) as their primary Federal regulators submitted 47 percent and 36 percent, respectively, of all mortgage loan fraud SARs from July 1, 2007 through June 30, 2008. In terms of total depository institutions, a third of filing institutions reported the Federal Deposit Insurance Corporation (FDIC) as their primary Federal regulator; however, the number of mortgage loan fraud SARs prepared by these filers was comparatively low. This shows that although mortgage loan fraud was suspected by depository institutions of all charter types, a subset of larger institutions chartered by the OCC and OTS accounted for the bulk of the SARs filed.

In the last year of the review period, filing institutions under the Federal supervision of OTS filed the most SARs with mortgage loan fraud as an activity characterization, submitting more than 29,000 such reports. Filing institutions under the supervision of OCC submitted the second largest volume, with nearly 22,000 such reports.[14]

---

13. The total *filings* should not be confused with the filing institutions' proportion of SARs on other *activities*, since SARs frequently indicate multiple activity characterizations.

14. Of the nearly 180,000 mortgage loan fraud SARs submitted between July 1, 2002 and June 30, 2008 which listed a primary Federal regulator, about one percent of all such reports did not provide the primary Federal regulator.

Chart 6 and Table 3 show yearly comparisons of total SARs with mortgage loan fraud as an activity characterization, grouped by the primary Federal regulator of the reporting institutions.

Chart 6

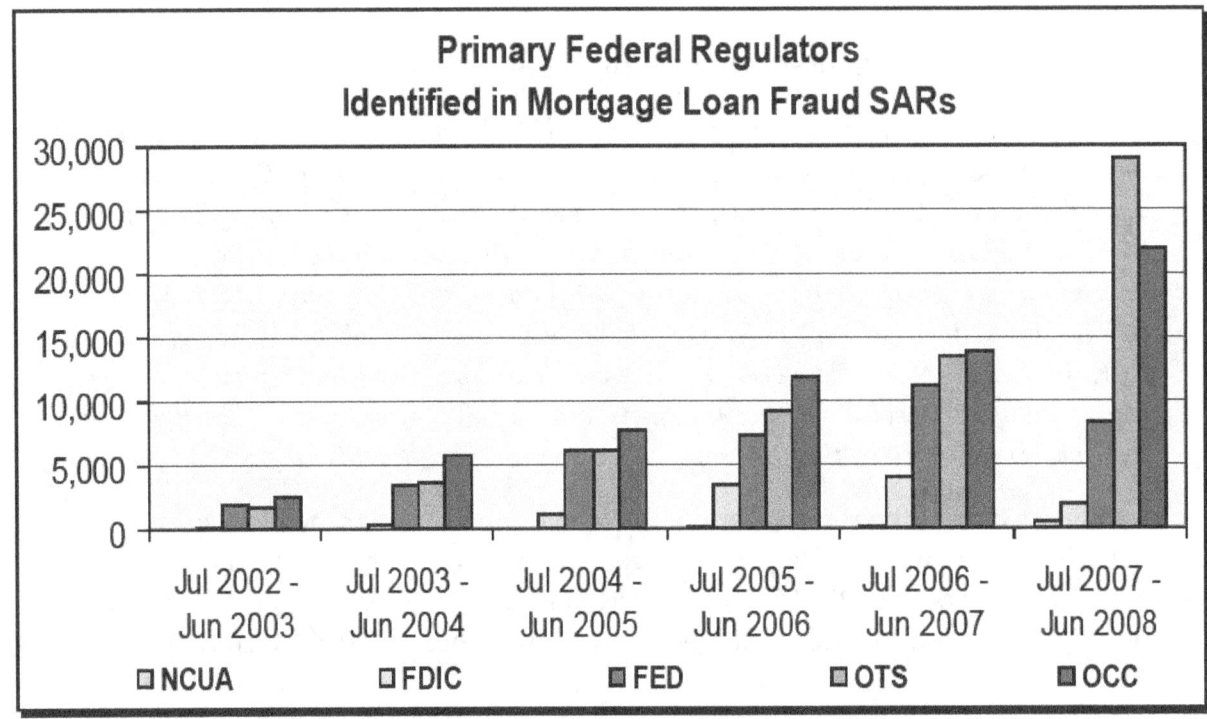

Table 3

Primary Federal Regulators Identified in Mortgage Loan Fraud SARs - Totals					
Filing Date Range	NCUA	FDIC	FED	OTS	OCC
Jul 2002 - Jun 2003	20	265	1,827	1,668	2,568
Jul 2003 - Jun 2004	36	391	3,447	3,645	5,786
Jul 2004 - Jun 2005	60	1,169	6,076	6,115	7,638
Jul 2005 - Jun 2006	107	3,506	7,266	9,170	12,007
Jul 2006 - Jun 2007	203	4,097	11,155	13,409	13,937
Jul 2007 - Jun 2008	541	1,928	8,277	29,023	21,974
Total	967	11,356	38,048	63,030	63,910

Table 4 shows the percentage (rounded) of these reports relative to the total of mortgage loan fraud SARs.

Table 4

Mortgage Loan Fraud SARs - Percentage Comparison of Reported Primary Federal Regulators					
Filing Date Range	NCUA	FDIC	FED	OTS	OCC
Jul 2002 - Jun 2003	<1%	4%	29%	26%	40%
Jul 2003 - Jun 2004	<1%	3%	26%	27%	43%
Jul 2004 - Jun 2005	<1%	6%	29%	29%	36%
Jul 2005 - Jun 2006	<1%	11%	23%	29%	37%
Jul 2006 - Jun 2007	<1%	10%	26%	31%	33%
Jul 2007 - Jun 2008	1%	3%	13%	47%	36%

Depository institutions reporting the FDIC as the primary Federal regulator comprised a third of all filing institutions reporting suspected mortgage loan fraud during the period July 1, 2007 to June 30, 2008.[15] These institutions ranked fourth in overall submissions of mortgage loan fraud SARs, submitting an average of six reports per filer. Institutions regulated by the OTS and OCC, on average, filed more than 100 mortgage loan fraud SARs each. Most of the top 25 filing institutions were chartered by either the OCC or OTS. *Chart 7* shows the number of regulated entities that filed mortgage loan fraud SARs by indicated supervisory agency during this period.

Chart 7

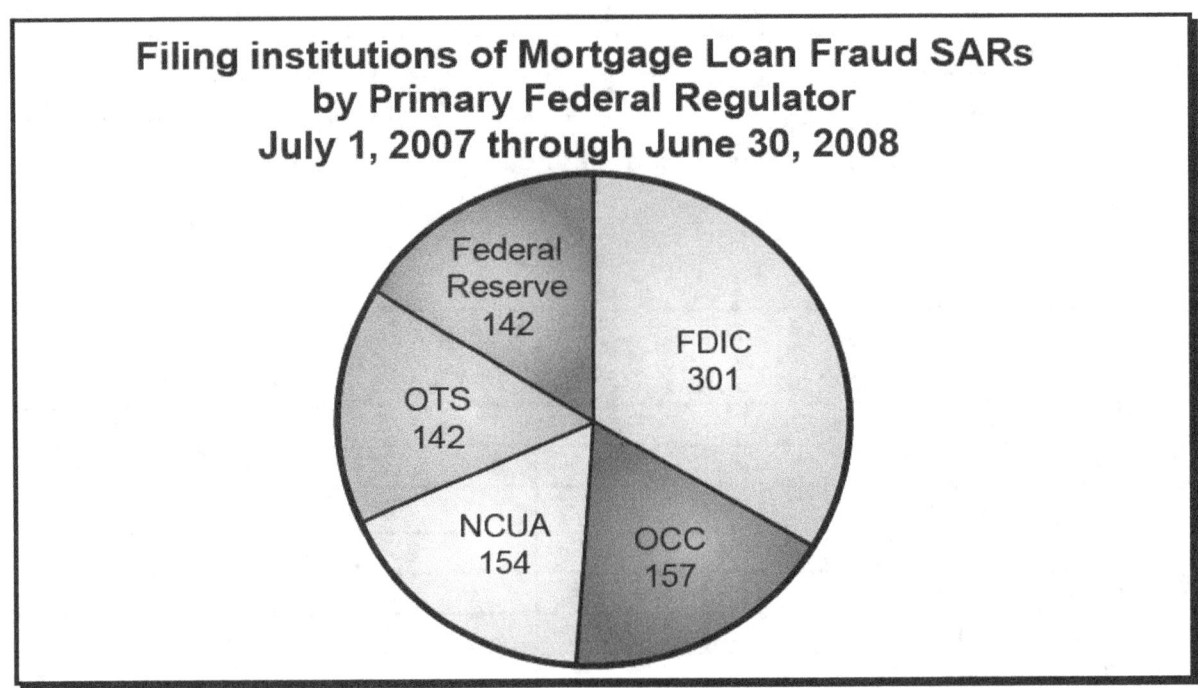

**Filing institutions of Mortgage Loan Fraud SARs
by Primary Federal Regulator
July 1, 2007 through June 30, 2008**

---

15. Filing institutions' self-reported EINs provide the basis for the counts of filing institutions. It is likely that the number of filing institutions is lower than the numbers provided due to data entry errors. Also, while the EIN represents a unique filing institution, it does not reflect the number of institutional affiliates that filed SARs on mortgage loan fraud, as some branches may use the same EIN.

Table 5 shows the average number of submissions for each filing institution based on the reported regulator.

Table 5

Mortgage Loan Fraud SARs: Average Number of Filer Submissions by Primary Federal Regulator July 1, 2007 to June 30, 2008	
Regulator	Average Number of Filer Submissions
NCUA	3
FDIC	5
Federal Reserve	56
OCC	136
OTS	182

Trends and Patterns in Activities Leading to Initial Suspicion

This final section describes the role of outside parties such as mortgage loan purchasers and providers of mortgage or certificate insurance and similar credit enhancement in identifying possible mortgage loan fraud.

Section Summary: A review of SAR narratives revealed that institutions detected possible mortgage loan fraud during the pre-funding stage of the loan in 34 percent of the filings. Filing institutions reported that repurchase demands and insurance investigations sometimes provided indications of potential mortgage loan fraud. Eight percent of the mortgage loan fraud SARs referenced repurchase agreements or demands, and another 8 percent referenced insurance; on average, these SARs were filed 7 months longer after the fraudulent activity than were all other mortgage loan fraud SARs. Narrative references in SARs to foreclosures and early defaults increased by 90 percent and 77 percent, respectively.

The sample group for this section included 1,050 SAR narratives describing the underlying activity. Parameters for the sample group included a 95 percent confidence level with a plus or minus three (+/-3) percent confidence interval. This review identified common filer terminology, usages and contexts for particular types of activities. Based on these findings, FinCEN analysts developed term searches to examine the other SAR narratives for similar patterns. In addition, the review helped to determine filing institutions' success rate at detecting fraud before funding loans.

Detection of Suspicious Activity Prior to Funding

FinCEN analysts reviewed the narratives of a representative sample of mortgage loan fraud SARs filed from July 1, 2007 through June 30, 2008 to determine the rate of detection pre- and post-funding. Filing institutions reported detecting possible fraud prior to funding loans in 34 percent of the reviewed SAR narratives.[16] This compares with the 31 percent rate for the 12-month period analyzed in FinCEN's April 2008 report, and the 21 percent rate over the preceding decade, showing that institutions have become increasingly vigilant in trying to protect themselves from and report suspected fraud.[17]

---

16. This figure excludes reports where analysts could not make a determination due to insufficient data.

17. *Mortgage Loan Fraud, An Update of Trends based Upon an Analysis of Suspicious Activity Reports,* April 2008, http://www.fincen.gov/news_room/rp/files/MortgageLoanFraudSARAssessment.pdf.

Contributing Factors Leading to Detection of Suspicious Activity

Filers often referenced certain types of events and information in depository institution SAR narratives as contributing to the institution's first indication of suspected mortgage loan fraud. Those included:

- Information provided to the filing institution when presented with a repurchase (sometimes referred to in the narrative as a "buy-back") request under the terms of a loan sale agreement;

- Information provided to the filing institution when notified by an insurer of an investigation arising out of a claim on an insurance policy;

- Information learned by the filing institution during the process of loan foreclosure proceedings; and

- Loans that became past-due and/or were in default.

Standard quality control reviews and enhanced fraud detection measures also appeared to be contributing factors in the detection of potential mortgage loan fraud.[18] In addition to lenders' discovery of potential mortgage fraud identified through their own internal processes, some filing institutions reported that these findings began with notifications from other institutions that were not involved in the origination of the loan(s) in question, such as buyers from the secondary market and providers of mortgage or certificate insurance and similar credit enhancement. Subsequent to receiving these notifications, many filing institutions made the decision to submit SARs reporting potential mortgage loan fraud.

Repurchase and Buy Back Demands

Mortgage loan sale agreements typically contain representations and warranties about the loans being sold, and sellers typically promise to repurchase any loan found to be in breach of these representations and warranties under specified circumstances and terms. One common representation and warranty gives the buyer the right to force the seller to buy back a loan that had fraud or specific misrepresentations involved in its origination. Filing institutions often referenced repurchase requirements and buy back demands in SAR narratives. Some of these narratives stated directly that the filing institution had received a demand from the buyer of a mortgage that the filing institution repurchase the mortgage on grounds of suspected fraud or misrepresentations. In the 12-month period ending June 30, 2008, filing

---

18. *Ibid.* For a fuller discussion of successful detection measures, see FinCEN's April 2008 report.

institutions mentioned "repurchase" or "buy back" in 8 percent of all mortgage loan fraud SARs. *Chart 8* shows the increase in SARs with narratives referencing repurchase or buy back demands.

Chart 8

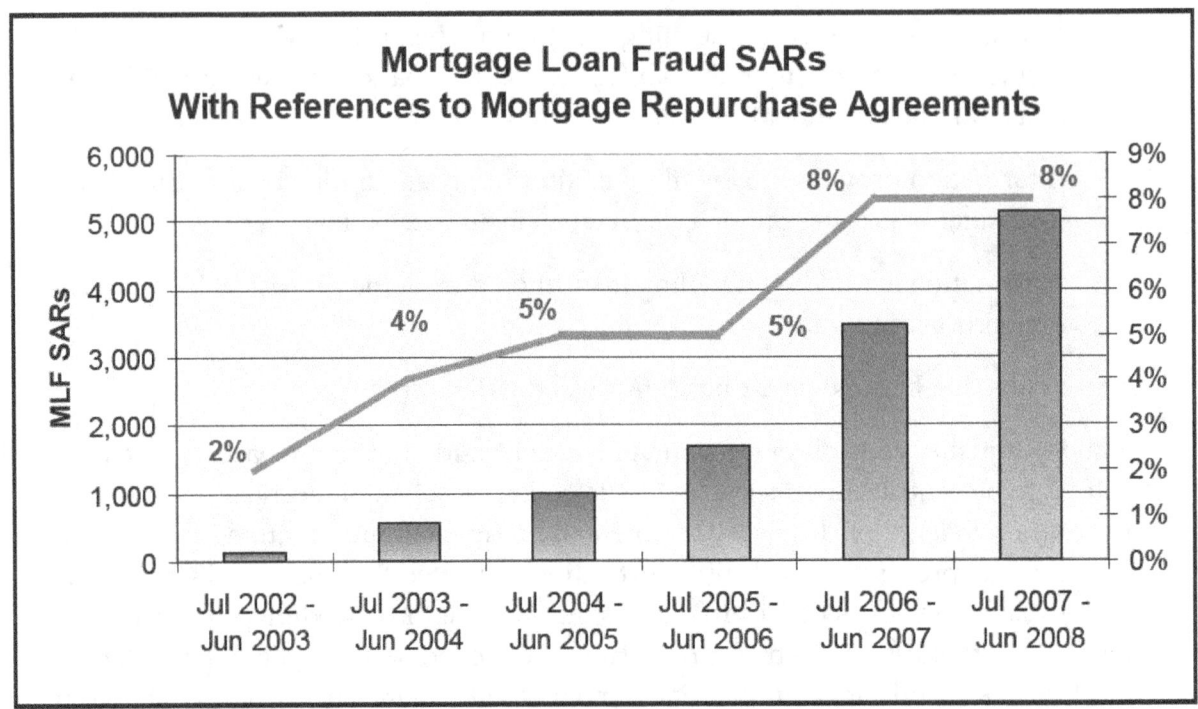

Two factors complicate efforts to quantify instances where buyers exercised repurchase demands due to fraud. First, many narratives referencing repurchase or buy back rights were ambiguous as to whether buyers actually exercised these rights. Second, in cases where buyers did clearly exercise these rights, the narrative often did not specify the reason for doing so. In these latter cases, buyers may have exercised their repurchase rights on grounds of fraud, but they may have called for a repurchase for other reasons, such as early defaults apparently unrelated to fraud.

In some mortgage loan fraud SARs referencing "repurchase," the reason for making this reference was clearly that the repurchase demand was the first indicator received by the filing institution that it should suspect possible fraud. Analysts attempted to determine whether repurchase demands were the principal reason for the filing of more than 5,000 mortgage loan fraud SARs, during the period from July 1, 2007 through June 30, 2008, that contained references to repurchase demands. Although these SARs did not provide enough information to determine *directly* if repurchase demands had prompted loan reviews by the loan originators leading to the detection of possible fraud, analysts developed an indirect test of the hypothesis.

Specifically, it could reasonably be expected that if a loan had been securitized and was only now the subject of a repurchase demand identifying possible fraud, which was now resulting in a SAR filing, then the time between the date of the loan and the SAR filing date[19] would be longer than it would be for SARs describing loans that had not undergone this process.[20] The analysis confirmed that this was the case, as mortgage loan fraud SARs with repurchase/buy-back references were filed on average 19 months after from the date the reported activity occurred, compared to an average filing time of 12 months for mortgage loan fraud SARs without such references.[21]

---

19. The SAR filing date is frequently later than the date the institution submitted the SAR. For this reason, the period between activity and filing dates represents a *maximum* amount of time for the detection of possible fraud.

20. For the sake of simplicity, this test assumed that mortgage loan fraud SARs without references to repurchase demands reflected either nonexistent or unexercised repurchase rights. However, it is more likely that some filers simply did not include this information. Consequently, it is likely that the difference in average filing times is actually greater than calculated.

21. SAR, Part III, Field 33. This hypothesis assumes Field 33 generally reflects the loan application or approval date.

Insurance

In addition to references to loan purchasers, some narratives reported that investigations by insurers provided their first indicators of potential fraud. Of the 1,050 mortgage loan fraud SARs reviewed, only a few clearly stated that the filing institution's first indication of potential fraud arose from insurance investigations. Other mortgage loan fraud SARs referenced insurers but did not elaborate on the role of the insurers in detecting the suspicious activity.

FinCEN analysts reviewed SARs to determine if the references to insurers indicated more than a standard reporting procedure. Fewer than 15 percent of filing institutions with SARs referencing insurers routinely made these references. Within this group of filers, only five submitted more than three mortgage loan fraud SARs. These findings suggest that the references are included for some other reason than standard institutional procedures for preparing mortgage loan fraud SARs. As in the case of mortgage loan fraud SARs referencing repurchases, SARs with references to insurers averaged 19 months between the activity and the SAR filing dates, compared to the average of 12 months between activity date and filing date for mortgage loan fraud SARs without these references.

Chart 9 illustrates the increase in narrative references to insurers.

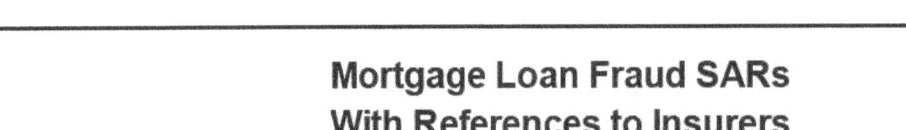

Chart 9

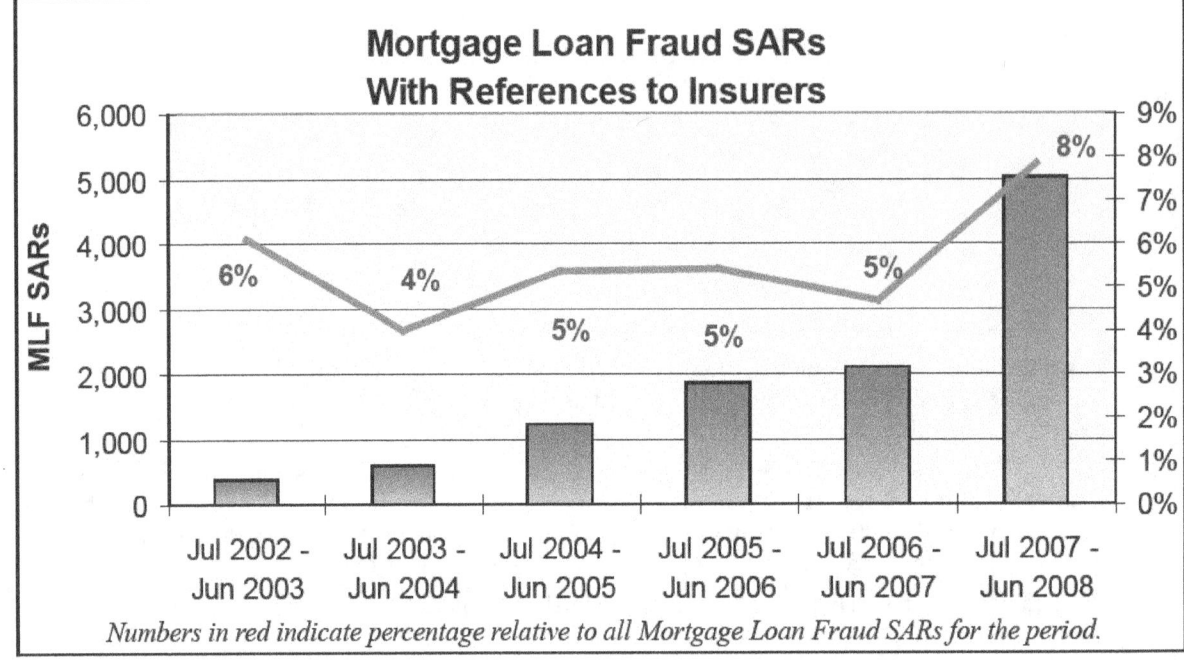

Foreclosures and Early Defaults

Factors such as foreclosure data also appeared to facilitate detection of suspected mortgage loan fraud. Since filers were often silent on the loan status, complete data was not available to determine the total number of reported activities that resulted in foreclosures and early defaults. *Table 6* identifies the number of SARs that included references to foreclosures and early defaults.

Table 6

Mortgage Loan Fraud SARs References to Foreclosures and Early Defaults				
	Foreclosures	*Increase*	*Early defaults*	*Increase*
Jul 02 - Jun 03	550		123	
Jul 03 - Jun 04	1,239	125%	150	22%
Jul 04 - Jun 05	2,452	98%	370	147%
Jul 05 - Jun 06	3,441	40%	581	57%
Jul 06 - Jun 07	4,162	21%	834	44%
Jul 07 - Jun 08	7,910	90%	1,478	77%

Next Steps

FinCEN will continue to monitor SARs to identify mortgage loan fraud trends. Forthcoming analyses will present information on reported subjects and activities. These assessments will examine the relationship between mortgage loan fraud and other financial fraud, and describe reported activities, locations, and subjects. In addition to commonly reported activities, these analyses will include greater information on identity theft, international connections, and related activities found in other BSA reports.

Financial Crimes Enforcement Network

U.S. Department of the Treasury

FinCEN is committed to distributing information to the public, financial industry professionals, and law enforcement professionals, in ways that can be readily found and used. We encourage feedback from readers on what information is of the greatest use. Your feedback is important and will assist us in planning future issues of FinCEN strategic analytical products. Please feel free to use this form, or provide your comments in the manner most convenient for you. The form can be faxed to FinCEN at (202)354-6411 or e-mailed to Webmaster@fincen.gov.

Please identify your type of financial institution.

Depository Institution:

__ Bank or Bank Holding Company

__ Savings Association

__ Credit Union

__ Edge & Agreement Corporation

__ Foreign Bank with U.S. Branches or Agencies

Securities and Futures Industry:

__ Securities Broker/Dealer

__Futures Commission Merchant

__Introducing Broker in Commodities

__Mutual Fund

Money Services Business:

__ Money Transmitter

__ Money Order Company or Agent

__ Traveler's Check Company or Agent

__ Currency Dealer or Exchanger

__ U.S. Postal Service __ Stored Value

Casino or Card Club:

__ Casino located in Nevada

__ Casino located outside of Nevada

__ Card Club

__ **Insurance Company**

__**Dealers in Precious Metals, Precious Stones or Jewels**

__**Other** (please identify): _____

Please identify your Federal or State regulatory agency

__Federal Deposit Insurance Corporation

__Federal Reserve Board

__National Credit Union Administration

__Office of the Comptroller of the Currency

__Office of Thrift Supervision

__Securities & Exchange Commission

__State Regulatory Agency – please identify_____

__Other Federal Regulatory Agency– please identify:_____

Please identify your Federal, State or Local Law Enforcement Agency:

_____

Please identify other Federal, State or Local agency:_____

What information in this report did you find the most helpful or interesting? Please explain why:

_____

_____

_____

_____

_____

What information did you find least helpful or interesting? Please explain why:

_____

_____

_____

_____

_____

What new topics, trends, or patterns in suspicious activity would you like to see addressed in future FinCEN analytical reports? Please be specific - Examples might include: in a particular geographic area; concerning a certain type of transaction or instrument; other hot topics, etc.

_____

_____

_____

_____

_____

_____

Other Comments?:

_____

_____

Please email Feedback Forms to:
Webmaster@fincen.gov.

Or fax to:
Financial Crimes Enforcement Network (FinCEN)
(202) 354-6411

Or mail to:
FinCEN
P.O. Box 39
Vienna, VA 22183

www.FinCEN.gov